DAVIDO

The law of the LANTERN

Introduction

In a world where material wealth often overshadows the pursuit of true happiness, there are those who defy the expectations set upon them and follow a different path. DavidO, an extraordinary Nigerian-born artist, personifies the transformative power of the human spirit when guided by the "law of the lantern." This book invites you to embark on an illuminating journey through the life of a man who, despite being born into privilege, sought a deeper purpose beyond material riches.

DavidO: Law of the Lantern takes you beyond the surface-level fame and glitz, delving into the heart and soul of a multifaceted individual. Within these pages, we unravel the captivating story of a talented artist who dared to challenge societal norms and carve his own destiny. The "law of the lantern" serves as the guiding principle that propelled him towards personal growth, creative fulfillment, and an unwavering pursuit of happiness.

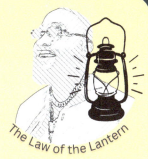

The Law of the Lantern

As you traverse DavidO's life, we begin by uncovering his background, immersing ourselves in the experiences that shaped his journey. From his early years, where the weight of his family's wealth cast shadows on his individuality, to the pivotal moment when he discovered music as his guiding light, you will witness the formation of a remarkable artist.

But this book is not solely about DavidO's rise to prominence; it is an exploration of the principles that guided him and can inspire us all. Through captivating storytelling, we navigate the highs and lows of his musical career, experiencing the impact of his unique sound on the world stage. We delve into the depths of his entrepreneurial ventures, as he creates opportunities for himself and others, leaving an indelible mark on the industry.

Beyond the music and success, the true essence of DavidO's story lies in the "law of the lantern." It is the profound realization that true fulfillment comes from aligning one's passions with purpose and finding joy in creating a positive impact. DavidO's journey serves as a powerful reminder that material wealth alone cannot fill the void within us—it is the pursuit of our dreams, the unwavering belief in ourselves, and the resilience to overcome obstacles that lead to genuine happiness.

In the pages that follow, we will delve into the intricacies of DavidO's life, highlighting his defining moments, his biggest achievements, and the lessons that can be extracted from his remarkable story. Each chapter will illuminate a different facet of his journey, guiding you to discover your own "law of the lantern" and inspiring you to live a life true to yourself.

So, prepare to be enthralled as we embark on this transformative odyssey. Together, let us embrace the spirit of DavidO: Law of the Lantern, and unlock the secrets to finding true happiness, creative fulfillment, and personal growth. As you turn the pages, may the light within you be kindled, leading you to forge your own extraordinary path.

Welcome to DavidO: Law of the Lantern. Let the journey begin.

So, dear reader, as we embark on this remarkable journey into the world of DaviO, let us open our hearts and minds to the wisdom he imparts. Let us embrace the law of the lantern as a guiding principle in our own lives, igniting the flames of passion, purpose, and happiness. Together, let us discover the extraordinary potential that lies within us all. Welcome to "DaviO: Law of the Lantern." Prepare to be inspired, transformed, and empowered to shine your light upon the world.

Table of Contents:

Chapter 1: Shadows of Privilege
1.1 The Power of Legacy
1.2 The Masked Struggles
1.3 The Call of Authenticity
1.4 The Tug of War
1.5 The Awakening

Chapter 2: A Melody Awakens
2.1 The Rhythm Within
2.2 Echoes of Inspiration
2.3 Striking the Chords of Resilience
2.4 The Art of Creation
2.5 Breaking Free with Sound
2.6 The Stage Beckons

Chapter 3: Rise to Stardom
3.1 The Breakthrough Hits
3.2 Igniting a Cultural Movement
3.3 Collaborations that Transcend Borders
3.4 Defying Industry Norms
3.5 The Impact Beyond Music

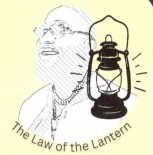

Chapter 4: Beyond the Spotlight
 4.1 The Birth of an Empire
 4.2 Fashion and Style: A Second Stage
 4.3 Giving Back: Impact and Philanthropy
 4.4 The Power of Influence
 4.5 Navigating the Challenges
 4.6 A Legacy Unparalleled

Chapter 5: The Law of the Lantern
 5.1 Illuminating the Path
 5.2 Finding Happiness Above All
 5.3 Lessons from the Journey
 5.4 Igniting the Lantern Within
 5.5 Illuminating Others: "We Rise by Lifting Others"
 5.6 The End is Just the Beginning

Chapter 1: Shadows of Privilege

1.1 In the Halls of Prosperity

Within the walls of opulence and prestige, the story of DavidO unfolds—a tale that weaves together the complexities of wealth, privilege, and the yearning for self-discovery. His journey commences against the backdrop of a family legacy steeped in success and affluence. Born into a lineage that commanded respect and
admiration, DavidO entered the world with a silver spoon in his mouth and the weight of great expectations upon his young shoulders.

1.2 The Veiled Burden

As a child, DavidO basked in the luxuries afforded
to him by his family's wealth. Lavish mansions, extravagant vacations, and a world of material abundance surrounded him. Yet, beneath the surface, there was an unspoken burden he carried— the burden of living up to the towering legacy left by his parents. Their triumphs and achievements loomed large, casting long shadows that threatened to overshadow his individuality.

1.3 A Desperate Quest for Identity

Growing up amidst abundance, DavidO's soul yearned for something more—a personal identity that extended beyond the confines of his family's wealth and reputation. As he navigated the
corridors of privilege, he felt a growing emptiness, a void that material possessions alone could not fill. The trappings of affluence seemed hollow in the absence of a deeper purpose, leaving him searching for a way to break free from the shackles of his upbringing.

1.4 The Clash of Expectations

Within the gilded halls of his family's domain, DavidO found himself entangled in a web of societal expectations. The world around him assumed that he would follow the prescribed path—upholding the family name, taking on the mantles of power and influence, and continuing the lineage of prosperity. Yet, his heart yearned for a different calling, a path that resonated with his own passions and dreams. The clash between tradition and personal authenticity waged within him, threatening to stifle his true potential.

1.5 An Unyielding Flame

Amidst the conflicting forces that tugged at him a flicker of resistance ignited within DavidO—a resolute refusal to be defined solely by his heritage. This inner flame grew brighter with each passing day, illuminating the path towards his own truth. With courage and determination, he embarked on a personal journey of self-discovery, seeking to unearth his unique identity and forge a legacy that was not confined to the expectations of others.

1.6 The Awakening

In a pivotal moment of awakening, DavidO stood at the precipice of transformation. He realized that to truly find fulfillment, he needed to shed the constraints of inherited privilege and embrace his own passions, dreams, and aspirations. The realization that true happiness lay beyond the confines of societal expectations set him on a path of liberation—a path that would lead him to his authentic self and illuminate the way towards the fulfillment of the "law of the lantern."

Chapter 2: A Melody Awakens

2.1 The Rhythm Within

Within the depths of DavidO's being, a dormant melody stirred, waiting to be awakened. It was a rhythm that resonated with his soul, a harmonious vibration that called out to him from the depths of his existence. As he embarked on his quest for self-discovery, music emerged as the catalyst through which he would find his voice, his purpose, and his place in the world.

2.2 Echoes of Inspiration

The seeds of DavidO's musical journey were sown amidst a tapestry of diverse influences. From the vibrant sounds of his Nigerian heritage to the intoxicating beats of global rhythms, his musical sensibilities were shaped by the echoes of inspiration that surrounded him. The richness of afrobeat, the soulful melodies of R&B, and the infectious energy of pop all became the building blocks upon which he would craft his unique sonic identity.

2.3 Striking the Chords of Resilience

A career in music is often accompanied by a symphony of challenges, and DavidO faced his fair share. In this chapter, we witness the struggles and setbacks that marked his early journey. Navigating the competitive music industry, facing initial rejections, and contending with self-doubt, he discovered the strength within himself to persevere. With every setback, he tuned his spirit to the chords of resilience, fortifying his determination to create his own destiny.

2.4 The Art of Creation

Within the sanctuary of recording studios and late-night jam sessions, DavidO found solace and purpose. It was in these sacred spaces that he honed his craft, unlocking the depths of his creativity. We delve into the process through which he breathed life into his music, exploring the delicate interplay between inspiration and dedication. Penning heartfelt lyrics, experimenting with melodies, and exploring the vast sonic landscape, he channeled his raw emotions into the art of creation.

2.5 Breaking Free with Sound

As DavidO's musical prowess blossomed, he discovered that his melodies possessed a transcendental power—a power to break free from the confines of his upbringing and touch the hearts of people across borders. Collaborations with international artists widened his sonic horizons, as he fearlessly fused cultural influences into his sound. Through his music, he became an ambassador of African creativity, unifying cultures and transcending boundaries with each beat.

2.6 The Stage Beckons

The stage became DavidO's canvas, where his artistry was unleashed upon the world. In this chapter, we witness the transformation that occurred as he stepped into the spotlight. With magnetic presence, he commanded the attention of audiences, captivating them with his electrifying performances. From intimate local venues to grand arenas, his stage presence radiated an energy that was contagious, leaving an indelible impression on all who experienced his musical magic.

Chapter 3: Rise to Stardom

3.1 The Breakthrough Hits

In the heart of DavidO's musical journey, a transformative moment awaited—an opportunity to break through the noise and capture the world's attention. This chapter chronicles the rise of DavidO's music as his breakthrough hits burst onto the scene. We witness the electrifying energy that surrounded the release of his early tracks, as the infectious rhythms and heartfelt lyrics resonated with audiences, propelling h
of stardom. im towards the precipice

3.2 Igniting a Cultural Movement

As DavidO's star began to ascend, his impact rippled beyond the realm of music. In this chapter, we explore how his unique sound became the catalyst for a cultural movement. Through his music, he ignited a newfound appreciation for Afrobeat, breathing new life into a genre deeply rooted in African heritage. The infectious beats and vibrant melodies captivated listeners worldwide, putting Nigerian music on the global map and opening doors for a new wave of African artists.

3.3 Collaborations that Transcend Borders

Collaborations became a cornerstone of DavidO's artistic journey, as he ventured beyond the boundaries of his own sound to forge connections with artists from around the world. This chapter delves into the transformative power of these collaborations, exploring the magic that unfolded when diverse musical voices intertwined. From iconic collaborations with international superstars to partnerships with rising talents, DavidO's music became a bridge that united cultures and showcased the beauty of artistic synergy.

3.4 Defying Industry Norms

In the pursuit of his artistic vision, DavidO fearlessly defied industry norms, carving out his own unique path. This chapter explores his innovative approaches to music-making, from experimenting with genre-blending to embracing unconventional release strategies. Through his entrepreneurial spirit, he disrupted the traditional music industry model and blazed a trail for artists to take control of their own careers, setting an example for a new generation of independent musicians.

3.5 The Impact Beyond Music

DavidO's influence extended far beyond the realm of music, and in this chapter, we explore the impact of his endeavors beyond the stage. From establishing his own record label to launching successful entrepreneurial ventures, he became a multi-faceted force in the entertainment industry. Additionally, his philanthropic efforts and commitment to social causes showcase his desire to create positive change in his community, leaving a lasting legacy that transcends his musical achievements.

3.6 The Evolution of a Star

As this chapter draws to a close, we witness the evolution of DavidO from a rising star to an icon. His journey is one of constant growth, adaptation, and unwavering dedication to his craft. From the breakthrough hits that catapulted him to fame to the global impact of his music and ventures, DavidO's ascent to stardom symbolizes the triumph of talent, resilience, and an unwavering belief in oneself.

Chapter 4: Beyond the Spotlight

4.1 The Birth of an Empire

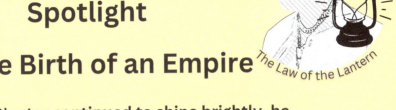

As DavidO's star continued to shine brightly, he transcended the boundaries of music and ventured into the realm of entrepreneurship. This chapter unveils the birth of an empire—a world where his creative vision extended beyond melodies and lyrics. We explore the establishment of his record label, the culmination of his entrepreneurial aspirations, and the platform he created to uplift and empower emerging artists in the industry.

4.2 Fashion and Style: A Second Stage

DavidO's influence expanded into the realm of fashion and style, becoming a trendsetter and icon in his own right. This chapter delves into his foray into the world of fashion, exploring the launch of his clothing line and the fusion of his personal style with his artistic persona. Through his fashion endeavors, he became a symbol of self-expression and individuality, inspiring others to embrace their unique identities.

4.3 Giving Back: Impact and Philanthropy

True greatness is measured not only by personal achievements but also by the positive impact one creates in the lives of others. In this chapter, we delve into DavidO's philanthropic endeavors, uncovering the ways in which he uses his influence to uplift communities and champion social causes. From charitable initiatives to supporting education and healthcare, his dedication to making a difference exemplifies his commitment to leaving a lasting legacy beyond the spotlight.

4.4 The Power of Influence

DavidO's ascent to stardom brought with it immense influence—a force that he wielded with great responsibility. This chapter explores how he harnessed his platform to effect change, becoming a voice for social justice, equality, and cultural appreciation. We examine the ways in which he used his influence to amplify underrepresented voices, challenge stereotypes, and foster a more inclusive and diverse industry.

4.5 Navigating the Challenges

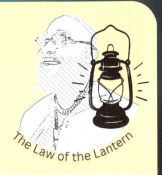

No journey is without its fair share of challenges, and this chapter delves into the obstacles that DavidO encountered on his path beyond the spotlight. From the pressures of fame and public scrutiny to the demands of managing a growing empire, we witness the resilience and determination that propelled him forward. Through the highs and lows, he remained steadfast in his pursuit of greatness, undeterred by the hurdles he faced.

4.6 A Legacy Unparalleled

As this chapter draws to a close, we reflect on the indelible legacy DavidO has created. His impact extends far beyond the realms of music, entrepreneurship, and philanthropy. It lies in the hearts of those he has inspired, the lives he has touched, and the transformative power of his journey. DavidO's story is a testament to the notion that true greatness lies not only in individual achievements but also in the ability to uplift others and leave a lasting impact on the world.

Chapter 5: The Law of the Lantern

5.1 Illuminating the Path

In the culmination of DavidO's extraordinary journey, we delve into the core essence of his story—the discovery and embodiment of the "law of the lantern." This chapter shines a light on the guiding principle that propelled him towards personal growth, happiness, and creative fulfillment. We unravel the profound wisdom hidden within his experiences, exploring how the law of the lantern can illuminate our own paths to happiness and success.

5.2 Finding Happiness Above All

DavidO's story is a testament to the truth that true happiness cannot be found solely in material wealth or societal expectations. This chapter delves into the moments when DavidO realized that genuine fulfillment resides in pursuing one's passions, staying true to oneself, and embracing the power of creativity. We explore how he broke free from the constraints of privilege and societal norms, forging his own path towards happiness and inspiring others to do the same.

5.3 Lessons from the Journey

Within the chapters of DavidO's life, valuable lessons are embedded, waiting to be discovered. In this chapter, we extract the pearls of wisdom that his journey offers. We reflect on the importance of authenticity, resilience, and determination, learning from DavidO's unwavering commitment to his dreams. We uncover the transformative power of self-belief, collaboration, and giving back, drawing inspiration from his unwavering spirit and his impact on the world.

5.4 Igniting the Lantern Within

As we journey alongside DavidO, we are invited to ignite our own lanterns—to tap into our passions, pursue happiness, and find our unique paths to fulfillment. This chapter guides us through the process of embracing our inner light, encouraging us to uncover our true purpose and live a life aligned with our deepest desires. Through the lens of DavidO's experiences, we gain insight into how we can apply the law of the lantern in our own lives.

5.5 Illuminating Others: "We Rise by Lifting Others"

The Law of the Lantern

At the heart of DavidO's story lies a powerful saying that has become synonymous with his journey: "We rise by lifting others." In this chapter, we explore how DavidO's commitment to lifting others up has shaped his impact on the world. We witness his dedication to supporting emerging artists, providing platforms for their voices to be heard and their talents to shine. We delve into his philanthropic endeavors, as he uses his success to uplift communities and ch ampion causes that are dear to his heart. Through his actions, DavidO exemplifies the belief that true greatness lies in the ability to make a positive impact on the lives of others.

5.6 The End is Just the Beginning

As this chapter draws to a close, we realize that the end of DavidO's story is not truly an end, but rather a new beginning—a beginning for readers to embark on their own journeys of self-discovery, growth, and happiness. The law of the lantern becomes a guiding principle

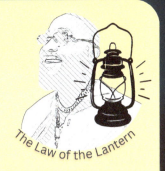

that transcends the pages of this book, inspiring us to unlock our potential, embrace our passions, and create our own paths to fulfillment. DavidO's story serves as a reminder that the power to transform our lives lies within us, waiting to be ignited.

Acknowledgments

I would like to extend my heartfelt gratitude to David Adedeji Adeleke, widely known as Davido, for being the inspiration behind this book. David, your unwavering commitment to using your platform to uplift and empower people both near and far has touched countless lives and served as a guiding light for many.

Your music, your philanthropic endeavors, and your dedication to making a positive impact have not only entertained audiences but have also created opportunities and sparked hope in communities around the world. Your belief in lifting others up, as exemplified in your powerful song "Stand Strong," has resonated deeply with me and has shaped the core message of this book—the law of the lantern.

I am grateful for your artistry, your authenticity, and your resilience. Your journey, marked by personal growth and a relentless pursuit of happiness and creative fulfillment, has inspired me and many others to embrace our own passions and strive for greatness. I would also like to express my gratitude to all those who have supported me throughout the writing process. To my friends, family, and mentors who have provided encouragement, guidance, and invaluable feedback, thank you for being a source of inspiration and strength.

To the readers of this book, I hope that the pages within transport you on a transformative journey, igniting your own lanterns of passion and purpose.

May the lessons from Davido's remarkable story empower you to embrace the light within, stand strong, and create your own path to happiness and success.
Thank you, Davido, for shining your light and for being a beacon of inspiration to us all.
With deepest appreciation,
Felix R Okafor

About the Author

The Law of the Lantern

Felix Raluchukwu Okafor is a passionate writer and a serving corps member in Enugu State, Nigeria, as of 2023. With an innate love for music and a keen interest in exploring the captivating stories of influential figures, Felix embarked on a journey to capture the essence of one such remarkable artist: DavidO.

Growing up with a deep admiration for artists who use their music as a powerful medium of expression, Felix's affinity for DavidO's character and artistry was ignited upon discovering the living legend. It was through the soul-stirring track titled "Stand Strong" that Felix was particularly drawn to DavidO's message of resilience, hope, and the power of standing tall in the face of challenges.

Felix's admiration for DavidO's music extends beyond mere appreciation; it evokes a profound connection reminiscent of the admiration felt for iconic artists like 2Pac. Witnessing the living legend in action, Felix found a renewed inspiration to delve deeper into the journey that shaped DavidO's remarkable rise to prominence. Driven by an ardent desire to share the story of an artist who has touched the lives of many, Felix embarked on the task of writing this book, exploring the complexities of DavidO's life, the lessons learned, and the law of the lantern that guided his path. As a writer, Felix is committed to capturing the essence of DavidO's journey, showcasing the transformative power of music, and inspiring readers to embrace their passions and rise above their circumstances.

The Law of the Lantern

Through his words, Felix aims to shine a light on the remarkable achievements and unwavering spirit of DavidO, inviting readers to embark on a journey of self-discovery, growth, and the pursuit of happiness.
It is with great enthusiasm and deep appreciation for the artistry of DavidO that Felix shares this book, hoping that it will serve as a testament to the enduring impact of music, the power of resilience, and the unwavering belief that greatness can be achieved by standing strong.

FELIX R OKAFOR

The Law of the Lantern

Printed in the USA
CPSIA information can be obtained
at www.ICGtesting.com
LVHW060709040624
782147LV00018B/7